Original title:

Sonnets in the Sequoia

Copyright © 2025 Creative Arts Management OÜ

All rights reserved.

Author: Fiona Harrington

ISBN HARDBACK: 978-1-80567-343-9

ISBN PAPERBACK: 978-1-80567-642-3

Heartbeats in the Hushed Heights

In forests tall where shadows play,
The squirrels chatter all the day.
They plot and scheme with such delight,
As acorns fall and take to flight.

The trees stand proud, old as the sun,
While birds around them have their fun.
A woodpecker taps a secret code,
As if to say, 'Come join the show!'

Each breeze that rustles through the leaves,
Makes every critter laugh and tease.
They dance and prance with carefree flair,
In nature's stage, a grand affair.

The canopy holds mysteries,
Like hidden jokes or silly keys.
With every branch, a chance to jest,
In heights above, they feel the best.

Legends Linger Among Leafy Giants

Among the trunks with wisdom vast,
Old legends fill the air so fast.
A rabbit with a top hat sighs,
While hedgehogs spin and wearate ties.

The owls provide their sage advice,
In riddles sprinkled with some spice.
They wink and nudge their feathered friends,
As giggles float on gentle winds.

While wise old trees sway side to side,
They can't help but laugh at jokes implied.
Each root holds tales of silly plight,
In moonlit glades, beneath the night.

Among the leaves where whispers creep,
The laughter echoes, loud and deep.
While eagles soar with mirthful grace,
The forest floor holds all the space.

Echoes of the Redwood Sky

In the forest where giants stand tall,
Squirrels gossip about the weather's call.
They argue fiercely, who can climb best,
While acorns rain down, they fail the test.

Beneath branches with stories to share,
A raccoon jokes, without a single care.
He wears a mask, thinks he's undercover,
But the owl just hoots, 'You're just a blunder!'

The breeze snickers, as it swirls around,
Tickling leaves, making laughter resound.
Each tree has a tale, but they can't compete,
With the antics of critters that run on their feet.

In shadows, a fox plays hide and seek,
With a deer who's shy, but a bit of a cheek.
As twilight descends, the stars wink up high,
It's a funny old world beneath the redwood sky.

Beneath the Canopy's Embrace

Beneath the green roof, the dances commence,
A chipmunk's misstep is quite the suspense.
He slips on a pinecone, creates a big fuss,
As laughter erupts, that's just how it is.

The caterpillar claims he's a butterfly,
With a grandiose dream, oh my, oh my!
His friends just roll over, laughing aloud,
'You need more than green to be in that crowd!'

A woodpecker drums like he's in a band,
Sets the rhythm, all creatures take a stand.
But the raccoon, out of time, makes a blunder,
With a wiggle and jiggle, he wreaks all the thunder.

As twilight approaches, the forest turns bright,
The jokes keep rolling, just feel the delight.
Each leaf that rustles shares giggles and glee,
In the patchwork of life, all fun's meant to be.

Trunks that Touch the Heavens

Up the trunks that break the clouds,
Trees are telling tales all loud.
A squirrel insists he's the king of the park,
While a crow just caws, 'You don't even bark!'

A wise old owl plays judge and referee,
'No kings today, just let it be free!'
The raccoons snicker, plotting their scheme,
To steal all the snacks, live out their dream.

In the shade of the branches, everything's bright,
A tortoise rolls by, avoiding the fright.
'Why rush?' he says, with a grin on his face,
'Life's just a journey, not a crazy race.'

As evening dances on dappled ground,
The forest erupts with laughter all around.
So when you wander where the tall ones dwell,
You'll find silly tales only nature can tell.

Shadows of the Timeless Forest

In the shadows where whispers play low,
A badger steals snacks, putting on quite a show.
With crumbs on his face, he dances with glee,
While the rabbits just chuckle, 'Oh, look at he!'

The mushrooms are tipsy, with stories so grand,
They sway to the rhythm, in this soft, leafy land.
A frog croaks a tune, adds flair to the sight,
While a snake performs tricks, oh what a night!

The raccoon disrupts, causing quite the mess,
His juggling of berries turns into distress.
But laughter erupts, like a bubbling stream,
In this curious world, not all is as it seems.

As moonlight spills over the forest floor,
Creatures unite, ready to explore.
Each shadow is magic, every giggle a spark,
In the timeless woods, where the fun leaves its mark.

Embraced by Nature's Majesty

Under grand canopies, we laugh and play,
Branches wave like arms in a gentle sway.
Squirrels chase each other, quite a sight,
While birds crack jokes in their feathered flight.

The trunks stand tall with a wise, old grin,
Listening closely, you can hear them spin.
Tales of the years gone by, so absurd,
As a raccoon giggles, looking quite disturbed.

Reverence Under the Canopy

Beneath the giant trees, we do bow down,
Among the critters, a quirky crowd found.
A deer in spectacles reads a fine book,
While a fox in a tie gets lost in the nook.

Oh, nature's council is quite the affair,
With trees offering wisdom and quite the flair.
Their leaves rustle softly, secrets they share,
Maybe they gossip, if only we care.

Tales of Twisting Roots

Twisted roots whisper as they trip and fall,
A tangled ball of jokes, they giggle and call.
The ground shakes a little, a dance now begins,
As worms wear top hats and grin silly grins.

With roots like fingers, they reach for the sun,
But watch your step – it could be quite fun!
Would you join the dance, or laugh from afar?
Nature's comedy show is truly bizarre.

Heartfelt Murmurs of Tall Trees

Tall trees do chuckle, their bark full of cheer,
Sharing sweet whispers that only we hear.
Branches sway lightly, secrets on the breeze,
While leaves laugh and flutter, tickled with ease.

They've seen silly things, oh do let them tell,
Of picnics gone wrong and squirrels that fell.
With a wink and a nod, they welcome us near,
In this nature's realm, there's nothing to fear.

Reflections in the Stillness of Wood

In the forest so grand and so wide,
Squirrels scurry, they just can't hide.
Trees whisper secrets with a cheeky grin,
I swear one winked at me—what a sin!

Moss covers rocks like a fluffy coat,
A snail just pondered, then started to float.
I chuckled aloud at the trees' little dance,
Each branch seemed eager to join in the chance.

In Awe of Nature's Monuments

Tall trunks stand proud, like ancient kings,
Waving their branches and all the good things.
A woodpecker pokes at a tree with flair,
Is he auditioning for a rockstar's air?

The roots hold tales from centuries past,
Their knots and gnarls, a history cast.
A deer just wandered with socks on his feet,
Yet still, he looked dapper—oh, what a treat!

Verses Amidst Verdant Peaks

Among the hills, the shadows just tease,
Each turn reveals a new set of trees.
Laughter echoes through the glades so bright,
As chipmunks debate which nut is just right.

Ferns dance around like they know the beat,
A chorus of foliage, oh, what a feat.
The sky looks down with a twinkle and laugh,
Nature's comedians, their own autograph.

Petals of the Forest Floor

A carpet of petals in colors galore,
Sprinkled with laughter from the forest's core.
Bees play tag with a butterfly fleet,
While ants strut by on their little street.

A mushroom threw a party one sunny day,
Tiny toadstools dressed up in a wild ballet.
The sun peeked in for a moment of fun,
Nature's big circus, oh, what a run!

Journey through the Tree-Laden Path

Beneath the giants, shadows play,
Squirrels race in a nutty fray.
Birds debate a silly song,
While branches sway and play along.

A turtle taking your sweet time,
Laughs at all with a joyful chime.
The raccoons wear a party hat,
As whispers dance with the breeze and chat.

Mossy carpets where fairies tread,
Ancient tales of the trees are spread.
But watch your step, it's slippery here,
Or you'll end up with a pinecone smear.

With every twist, the path does wend,
Laughter in the air, on that you can depend.
Let's frolic in this leafy maze,
In nature's playground, we'll spend our days.

Bark-scribed Dreams

Underneath the mossy crown,
The trees embrace with laughter's sound.
Each imprint tells a quirky tale,
Of wooden laughs in the evening pale.

Bark bears witness to sweet romance,
Scribbled hearts in a wobbly dance.
While squirrels maneuver with sneaky grace,
To snag a kiss from the nutty space.

Branches gossip, leaves chime in,
With tales of fungi and sly chagrin.
If trees could chuckle, oh what a sound,
Echoes of giggles all around.

So let us carve our dreams in bark,
Not with knives, but with cheerful spark.
For in this forest, we craft our schemes,
And all our laughter forms bark-scribed dreams.

The Language of Leaves

Rustling whispers, secrets sway,
As leaves giggle in the sun's warm play.
Each flutter has a tale to weave,
In the silly dance of the autumn eave.

With every gust, they flutter down,
A shower of laughter on the frowning crown.
Conversations between buds and twigs,
About the joys of winter digs.

The oak tells jokes, the willow sighs,
While poplars roll their leafy eyes.
In every rustle, there's wit to find,
Nature's comedy, perfectly aligned.

So join the chat in this leafy spree,
And learn the jests of the old cedar tree.
For in the language of leaves we see,
The humor printed in green jubilee.

An Ode to the Earth's Canopy

Oh canopy high, with branches spread,
We giggle and sway, like candy in thread.
Swaying in rhythm, the branches unite,
A ticklish tick-tock, such sheer delight.

The clouds like marshmallows drift on by,
Occasional rain, like a sweet pie sky.
Beneath your boughs, the critters play,
In the shade where the shadows laugh all day.

Your leafy laughter, a joyous refrain,
Bringing happiness in every rain.
As acorns fall with a playful plop,
Nature's jesters in a never-ending backdrop.

So here's to you, oh great green dome,
For making the wild a whimsical home.
In the embrace of your leafy guise,
We celebrate life with laughter that flies.

Vows Under the Arches of Leaves

We promised under leaves so tall,
To love each other through it all.
But when it rains upon our heads,
We laugh till we're as wet as beds!

The squirrels witnessed our grand show,
They thought our vows were quite the go.
With nutty giggles in the breeze,
We sealed our love with heartfelt wheeze!

If branches bend, we'll navigate,
And dance around when things are late.
For life's a jest, and so we cheer,
Our love grows strong, year after year!

So here we stand, beneath this tree,
Correlating love with glee.
As long as laughter lights our path,
We'll toast to joy, and love, and math!

Light's Dance Through Ancient Boughs

The sunlight twinkles like a wit,
It plays with shadows, just for kicks.
A game of tag, it runs and flies,
While ancient trees all roll their eyes!

We spin like leaves on autumn's breeze,
And joke about the busy bees.
With every step, we hear them hum,
Their buzz a tune—fun's never dumb!

The branches sway with quirk and flair,
As if they've just grown legs to share.
With each step, we both laugh and shout,
These ancient woods know what's it's about!

Let's dance beneath this leafy dome,
And turn this forest into home.
With wit as sharp as bark-worn grooves,
Our love, like dancing light, removes!

Forests as Living Testaments

In woods where age defies the clock,
We stroll through time like a funny flock.
Each tree a witness with a grin,
To tales of love where we begin!

The trunks stand tall, a leafy crowd,
They chuckle softly, quite unbowed.
With every whisper, secrets shared,
A love that's bold, a bond declared!

We'll climb the branches, feel the height,
As branches bend, we hold on tight.
With laughter echoed on each leaf,
We conquer woods with joyous belief!

With roots like vows, we intertwine,
A comical love, oh so divine.
As forests sway to life's sweet jest,
Our love will soar, and we'll be blessed!

Whispers of Woodland Love

The leaves conspire, they gossip fast,
With stories old that hold us fast.
They tell of lovers brave and bold,
Amongst the branches, tales retold.

A critter passing rods us sly,
With twinkling eyes to glance and pry.
"Is that a date or just a game?"
It winks at us—oh, what a shame!

Each rustling leaf a playful jest,
Reminds us that we are the best.
Through laughter shared between the trees,
We love with all the woodland's ease!

So let them whisper, let them sing,
To every petal, heart takes wing.
In woodland corners, love is free,
With chuckles bright as we can be!

Hushed Confessions of Timeworn Trees

In whispers soft, the branches sway,
They gossip 'bout the birdies' play.
With rings of age, they share a jest,
A comedy of roots, the oldest, best.

A squirrel has claimed the highest throne,
While acorns drop like seeds of bone.
They chuckle at the rustling breeze,
As shadows dance on bended knees.

Old trunks, like grandpa, stand so wise,
With knobbly knees and wrinkled sighs.
When falling leaves start their slow waltz,
They share their tales of growth and faults.

With twilight's glow, they stretch and yawn,
Recalling evenings on the lawn.
In sleepy slumber, they crack a grin,
For every dawn, anew begins.

Infinity in the Groves

In endless rows, the giants sway,
Chasing shadows at the end of day.
With bark so thick, they crack a grin,
At tiny critters scurrying in.

Their branches sigh, a rustling glee,
As they bemock the busy bee.
The nights grow long, the jokes grow wide,
While stars above are their guide.

A woodpecker knocks with style and flair,
Declaring, "I'm the king, beware!"
The trees just chuckle, rooted deep,
In funny tales that never sleep.

So gather near, and lend an ear,
To secrets whispered far and near.
For in this grove, the laughter flows,
In echoes soft, where fun surely grows.

Reverie Among Great Behemoths

Among the giants, laughter rings,
In quiet tales, the joy it brings.
With gentle nods and creaky creaks,
The earth beneath them giggles and squeaks.

Roots entwined in a playful tease,
They swap their stories with the breeze.
While moss adorns their timeworn skin,
They joke about the years they've been.

"Oh look, a chipmunk hosting a feast!
A nutty banquet, not for the beast!"
In every fold, a tale unfolds,
Of silly moments gradually told.

As moonlight drapes their verdant heads,
In nighttime chats, the laughter spreads.
For amongst these towers, tall and grand,
A merry heart is always planned.

Heartstrings in the Heartwood

Deep in the wood, where laughter thrives,
The heartstrings twine, a joy that jives.
With roots that tickle and branches that sway,
The trees play pranks, come join the play.

A woodchuck struts in fanciful dress,
While beetles dance in a humorous press.
They share their secrets, bark to bark,
In moonlit whispers, they leave a mark.

When breezes laugh and squirrels tease,
The air is filled with fun-filled ease.
As shadows flicker and twirls abound,
In the heartwood's core, joy's always found.

So gather 'round, be merry and light,
For every laugh trips the dark of night.
Amidst the behemoths, old and wise,
Lies a spirit bright, in playful guise.

Echoing Timbers in Dusk's Lullaby

In the woods where whispers creep,
Trees gossip, secrets they keep.
Branches moan with tales of yore,
Leaves chuckle, who could ask for more?

Squirrels prance in twilight's glow,
Chasing shadows, putting on a show.
With acorns tossed like flying pies,
They giggle beneath the twilight skies.

Night descends with a gentle sigh,
A raccoon winks, oh me, oh my!
The moon's a spotlight on the scene,
Nature's circus, bright and keen.

When stars appear, the critters dance,
Taking turns in a merry prance.
Underneath this canopy wide,
Laughter echoes, what a ride!

A Tapestry of Green and Gold

In a forest dressed in shades so bright,
Frogs croak jokes, what a silly sight!
Dancing ferns in a breezy song,
Nature plucks strings all day long.

The sunbeams play hide and seek,
With raindrops giggling on a creek.
Bumblebees buzz with a tune in mind,
Pollinating joy, oh so entwined.

Trees wear crowns of leafy hats,
While owls debate the silliest chats.
"Who's wiser?" they hoot, "You or I?"
As squirrels just roll, "Let's eat and fly!"

Nature's quilt with threads of fun,
Stitching laughter 'til the day is done.
With every leaf, a hearty cheer,
A tapestry spun with wit and cheer!

Secrets Woven in Root and Sky

Roots of trees hold tales untold,
Of lovesick bugs and dreams of old.
A spider spins webs with a flair,
Crafting puns in the morning air.

Above, a bird tries to recite,
Poems that tickle with pure delight.
But a floppy worm coos, "Can't you see?
I'm the one that's truly free!"

Clouds drift by with a giggle or two,
Draping the blue in a cottony hue.
While boulders laugh, as they stand still,
"You shimmy and shake, but I'm quite a thrill!"

As stars shine in a velvet night,
Fireflies twinkle, bringing light.
In this realm of jest and cheer,
Nature's comedy draws all near!

Twilight Elegy of the Canopy

In dusk's embrace, the branches sway,
A chorus of critters starts to play.
Bats swoop low with a mischievous glee,
"How do you catch a flying bee?"

Below, raccoons in masks unite,
Planning escapades until the night.
They'll raid the picnic, make a scene,
It's the funniest heist you've ever seen!

Owls convene, wise and astute,
Debating who's got the best loot.
While fireflies flash in a whimsical race,
"Catch me if you can, just keep the pace!"

As twilight dances, the forest laughs,
With jokes and jests filling the paths.
In this elegy, joy takes flight,
Underneath the stars, so bright!

Dreams of Light Among the Timber

Beneath the tall trees, I often dream,
Of squirrels in suits with a grander theme.
They hold fancy parties, with acorns in hand,
Dancing on branches, the best in the land.

I wonder if chipmunks wear hats made of grass,
Or if the wise owl prefers sipping sass.
With laughter that echoes through leaves and through bark,
They tell jokes about humans who tread in the dark.

The sunlight peeks through, a spotlight so bright,
On critters with talent, all ready to smite.
They juggle with pinecones, a hilarious sight,
While debating if winter is worth the cold bite.

So next time you wander where tall timber sways,
Remember the humor in nature's grand play.
The trees stand so proud, with their long, leafy arms,
Embracing the joy which forever charms.

The Heartbeat of the Evergreen

The ferns gossip quietly, their stories so grand,
While the saplings conspire with brushes of hand.
They whisper sweet secrets of nature's delight,
Of pine-scented summers and snowflakes so light.

A raccoon in pajamas walks up to a tree,
He claims he's the king; it's a sight to see!
With laughter and mischief, he rules from his throne,
In a patch of wildflowers he claims as his own.

Underneath all the boughs, it's a carnival scene,
Where butterflies twirl in a dance so pristine.
The mossy old roots join a conga parade,
While crickets compose a sweet serenade.

And when the sun sets, it's a fiesta, for sure,
As shadows grow longer, and soft breezes stir.
So lift up a branch and join in the fun,
In the heart of the forest, where laughter's begun.

Whispers of Ancient Giants

Amidst towering giants, with shadows so great,
The trees share their laughter, a comical fate.
With knots and with gnarls, their faces will grin,
As they tell tales of how fun it's been.

The wind ticks and tocks, like a curious clock,
While branches break out in a waltz and a rock.
The roots stretch for miles in a twisty embrace,
In a game of charades, they've all found their space.

"Who's taller?" they argue, with roots all entwined,
With jokes about eagles, oh, they've lost their mind!
The squirrels don mustaches for a chuckle or two,
They claim it's a festival, just for the view.

So come take a journey through laughter and cheer,
Among these old sentinels, season to year.
In the whispers of giants, the tales will delight,
With humor that glimmers like stars in the night.

Arboreal Musings Under Starlight

In the woods, the squirrels plot,
Counting acorns, quite a lot.
With every nut, they cheer and dance,
In their world, they take a chance.

Owls hoot softly, night's choir thins,
While rabbits wear their tiny grins.
Mice sneak snacks from under trees,
A culinary heist with the breeze.

Above, the moon spills silver light,
As the fox tries to steal a bite.
The branches sway, a gentle tease,
Nature's jest, if you please.

So here we laugh, beneath the stars,
A kingdom full of tiny czars.
Amidst the foliage, we unite,
In this arboreal delight.

Chronicles of the Great Trees

Tall sentinels with leafy crowns,
Whisper secrets, wear old gowns.
Beneath their watch, we jest and play,
Sharing stories of the day.

The raccoons, dressed in masks so fine,
Plot their heists, sipping on brine.
While squirrels drape in autumn hues,
Wearing coats of red and blues.

The woodpecker, with rhythmic note,
Plays the tree like a fine old goat.
Each knock a joke, a hearty laugh,
Teaching trees to photograph.

As clouds drift by, we spin our tales,
Of furry friends and hidden trails.
In this grove where antics reign,
We find joy in nature's domain.

Sylvan Verses of Light and Shade

In the glade where shadows fall,
Laughter echoes, nature's call.
Deer prance by with graceful leaps,
Hiding secrets that the forest keeps.

Frogs croak sonnets by the stream,
While crickets form a night-time dream.
Fireflies twinkle like tiny stars,
Laughing at their own wayward cars.

An old badger tells a tale or two,
Of mischief made in morning dew.
And chipmunks join with cheeky flair,
Sharing snacks without a care.

Underneath the emerald dome,
Creatures make this forest home.
With jokes and jests, we intertwine,
In this realm, our hearts align.

The Language of Tall Shadows

Tall shadows stretch and sway at dusk,
Creating shapes, revealing husk.
A parrot squawks at the setting sun,
Declaring that the day was fun.

The bumblebees buzz with laughter sweet,
Dancing round the flowers in fleet.
While tortoises take their slow strolls,
Waving at frogs with lofty goals.

The trees hold secrets in their bark,
Whispered jokes from dusk till dark.
As night falls down with a gentle hush,
The forest glimmers, in quiet rush.

So linger here, beneath the moon,
With nature's laughter, a joyous tune.
For every leaf tells tales anew,
In this whimsical, leafy view.

Love Letters to the Majestic Trees

Oh mighty tree, with bark so rough,
Your leaves are green, but that's not enough.
I write you notes that rustle with glee,
Hoping you'll send some whispers to me.

In spring you sprout like a wild hairdo,
And squirrels take bets on what you will do.
You sway and dance in the breeze so fine,
Even the birds stop to sip on your wine.

Your roots stretch out, like feet in a shoe,
Grabbing at secrets that only you knew.
Dear tree, you're a giant with heart so free,
Can I be your shadow? Just let it be me.

When winter comes, oh how you will freeze,
I'll knit you a sweater, if you please!
For all your height, you still feel the cold,
So take this love—let our story be told!

Sentinels of the Whispering Woods

In the forest's hush, where silence reigns,
Stand tall and proud, those leafy remains.
With whispers soft like secrets untold,
They crack jokes about the ancient and old.

I caught a tree giggling, oh so sly,
As a beetle slipped past on a twig high.
"Timber!" it yelled, "But not on my watch!"
And the whole lot shook—Oh what a botch!

Beneath your boughs, I've tripped and I've stumbled,
You laughed as I tumbled, and then I grumbled.
Your bark's full of laughter, it's plain to see,
At least I'm not Chuck, who fell from a tree!

So let's toast to trees, the tall and the wide,
Whispering wisdom, our sturdy guide.
With every quip and every wise crack,
You make forest life a lovely whack!

Heartbeats of an Ancient Grove

In the grove where the big ones sway,
They tell tall tales in their own way.
With trunks so thick and spans so wide,
They mock my height—oh great tree pride!

One said, "Hey, you'll never reach my crown,
Don't try to climb, just sit down, clown!"
They all chuckled, a deep woody laugh,
While I plotted my climb—my tree-bound path.

Underneath, a parade of leaves,
Tickle my nose, oh how nature thieves.
You think you're so grand, with your leafy crown,
But I'll bring you cookies—I'll take you down!

So here's a cheer to all you old trees,
With heartbeats soft in the teasing breeze.
I seek your wisdom, your jokes full of glee,
Just don't mind my snickers—listen to me!

Roots that Reach for the Past

Roots that dig deep, what do you know?
Hiding from sunlight, putting on a show.
You twist and you turn as you reach all around,
Gossiping with rocks—what secrets abound?

"Hey there, buddy! I know you were there,
You were a pebble, now you're quite rare!"
They laugh at the squirrels, they chuckle as they play,
And weave funny stories of old trees' heyday.

With limbs that extend, like arms to embrace,
They hold all the laughter—the woodpecker race.
A tree with a mustache said, "Take a look here,
These comics of nature will bring you some cheer!"

So let's celebrate roots that reach and entwine,
The past speaks in riddles with each twist in line.
With every wise crack that flows through the leaves,
I'll dance with the trees, sharing heights of our eves!

Ode to the Wooden Giants

Oh mighty trees, so tall and grand,
Your bark so rough, like seasoned sand.
With squirrels prancing all around,
You stand so proud, never falling down.

In your shade, a picnic we spread,
With ants performing their ballet instead.
You whisper secrets in the breeze,
While I just hope for snacks and cheese!

Your branches stretch, like arms in cheer,
But watch out for that bird, my dear!
In nature's comedy, we play our parts,
With laughter shared amongst our hearts.

So here's to you, old wooden friends,
With laughter our joyous song transcends.
May you waltz through time, so wise and spry,
While we giggle beneath the open sky.

Dreaming Beneath Towering Trunks

Beneath your shade, I take a nap,
Awake to find a raccoon's cap.
You stand so tall, but I'm not alone,
For in your roots, the gnomes are grown!

Your branches wave like silly hands,
As critters dance in little bands.
A woodpecker knocks, it's quite a show,
While I ponder if trees like disco!

In whispers soft, you drop your leaves,
Like nature's confetti, oh how it weaves.
I chuckle at squirrels, such clever thieves,
As they scurry about, with nuts up their sleeves!

So here I lie, 'neath trunk so wide,
In dreams of laughter, I gladly glide.
Till twilight falls and stars take flight,
I'll dream of trees, and all things bright.

Lament of the Woodland Spirits

In the grove where shadows play,
The spirits sigh, in disarray.
For every bark that seems to creak,
Is just a secret they can't speak.

They rustle leaves with a gentle moan,
"Hush now, don't interrupt our drone!"
With fairy lights and whispers shy,
They dance around, and we just sigh.

But what of elves, with shoes so green,
Who trip on roots, it's quite the scene!
"We're meant to fly, not fall or flop,
These ancient trees just make us stop!"

Yet in their laughter, spirits find grace,
In nature's circus, they take their place.
With giggles echoing through the night,
The forest shakes with pure delight.

Murmurs from the Noble Grove

In the noble grove, the stories flow,
Of playful winds that flutter so.
Each branch a tale, each twig a laugh,
Of critters plotting a cheeky gaffe.

"Ouch!" cries an owl, too quick to swoop,
As a wayward squirrel dives in a loop.
With giggles hiding in the rustling leaves,
Nature's humor is what she weaves.

From the mossy floor to the lofty heights,
The trees chuckle at nightly sights.
"Do you hear that?" whispers the breeze,
"Another party, come join with ease!"

So raise a toast to the playful glade,
Where laughter blooms in every shade.
With hearts so light, we find our groove,
In the woodland's whispers, we all move.

Soliloquy Among the Sundrenched Foliage

In the shade of leaves so grand,
I ponder life with the squirrels' band.
They chatter on about their stash,
While I sit here without a dash.

The sunbeams dance through branches thick,
I try to join, but lose my trick.
The birds all laugh, so high above,
While I just wish for some sweet love.

A chipmunk winks, then runs away,
I hear his giggles, 'Guess I'll stay.'
With every rustle, I can hear,
Nature's humor rings so clear.

As leaves drop down in playful grace,
I try to catch them in the race.
But, oh dear me, they all just glide,
While I fall flat and just abide.

Threads of Time in Timbered Heights

Amidst the giants, I do prance,
Life's a quirky, nature dance.
A beetle rolls a tiny ball,
While I just trip and take a fall.

The woodpecker gives me a stare,
Does he think I'm unaware?
With pecks so rhythmic, sound so bright,
I jam while he's in perfect flight.

The sun can't help but tickle leaves,
And tricking me, it steals and weaves.
I chase the shadows, but they run,
As laughter echoes, all in fun.

I find a knot to have a seat,
And laugh at life, oh what a treat!
With trees that chatter, all in jest,
I wave goodbye, but I'm not blessed.

Poems in the Lattice of Branches

In twirling shadows, verses spin,
With playful words, let's all begin.
A wise old crow might just critique,
But his ruffled feathers are so bleak.

A squirrel drops by to share a tale,
Of acorns lost upon the trail.
I ponder hard, pretending wise,
He chuckles loud, with bright, sly eyes.

The sunlight weaves through leafy grids,
While I compose my thoughts like kids.
The owls hoot softly, judging me,
And giggles rise like honeybee.

With each new stanza, branches sway,
As laughter echoes through the day.
The trees, they giggle, whisper low,
As I pen verses in the glow.

Starlit Conversations with Titans

Beneath the sky, where shadows play,
I chat with titans in dismay.
They whisper secrets, old and wise,
I stumble back, with wide-open eyes.

The stars giggle with twinkling grace,
As I try hard to keep my pace.
A raccoon laughs, with mask so sly,
'You'll never catch them, oh, so spry!'

With tales of glory, trees grow tall,
I stand enthralled, beneath it all.
Their bark is humor, thick and strong,
While I just plod and hum along.

When night gives way to morning light,
The giants beam, such a bright sight.
I wave them off, with joy and cheer,
For tomorrow's chatter draws me near.

Harmony Beneath the Fortress of Green

In the shade, the squirrels play,
Chasing shadows, come what may.
Beneath the branches, giggles rise,
As birds drop seeds from sunny skies.

A picnic's mishap, crumbs galore,
Ants march in like they own the floor.
A dance of leaves in the gentle breeze,
Nature's jesters, bringing us ease.

The trees, they gossip about the sun,
With barky chuckles, oh what fun!
Each whisper wraps around the roots,
While nature's silly jubilee hoots.

And as we nap, a soft thud lands,
A pine cone drops, just like it planned.
Echoes of laughter in every glen,
Harmony found, until then!

Treetops and Tenderness

At dawn, the owls start to yodel,
While squirrels wear socks, what a model!
The leaf parade begins to sway,
In this treetop cabaret, we play.

With twiggy hats, the robins sing,
Fluffy tails, the foxes bling.
Underneath this leafy dome,
Every creature feels at home.

An acorn fell right on my head,
Nature's joke? I think it said!
The woodpecker's tap is quite the beat,
Drumming up friends for a mighty feat.

"Join us up here, the view is grand!"
A ladder of branches, oh, so planned.
The laughter climbs to skies so bright,
Where treetops meet in pure delight.

Breathing in the Age of Giants

In a world where giants stand tall,
Pine needles rain like confetti fall.
A chipmunk's stash, serious business,
Yet every snack's a giggling witness.

A lumbering bear yawns quite wide,
While playing peek-a-boo, we must hide.
"Is that a berry or a bumbling snack?"
Dreamers in trouble, always in lack.

As mist floats by, a silly squirrel,
Ponders donuts in a dancy whirl.
While whispers tickle the ferns below,
All is well in this cheery show.

So let us breathe, and let us cheer,
With laughter louder than we hear.
In the age of giants, we all belong,
With funny tales in nature's song.

The Palpable Poetry of Nature

Among the roots, a poet spied,
A dancing leaf, nature's pride.
With whispers loud and giggles bright,
Wonders sprout, a pure delight.

A fox is rhyming with a mouse,
In the nooks of a tiny house.
"Shall we dance?" asks the butterfly,
With colors bright, it flits and flies.

The river sings its babbling tune,
While frogs perform beneath the moon.
Each ripple frames a joyous jest,
Nature's poem, at its best.

So come and join this lively spree,
Under the vast and daring tree.
With laughter spilling from every grove,
The palpable verse of nature's love.

The Dance of Leaves and Light

Leaves twirl in the breeze,
Dancing like no one sees.
Sunlight winks through the trees,
Nature's giggles, if you please.

Shadows stretch and weave,
In a playful autumn eve.
Branches sway and heave,
As if the woods believe.

Misty laughter fills the air,
Bark faces, oh, what a pair!
Trees plotting without a care,
In this woodland, humor rare.

Roots tickle the forest floor,
Whisper tales from years of yore.
Nature's jesters, forevermore,
In the light, we can't ignore.

The Timeless Dialogue of Branches

Branches gossip day and night,
Swapping stories, what a sight!
One claims a squirrel's great flight,
While another chuckles in delight.

"Did you see that bird's last flail?"
"Oh yes, it was a comical tale!"
With each sway, the laughter's gale,
In this forest, they shall prevail.

Indigo skies roll on with glee,
As leaves join in the revelry.
Chatty trunks, what joy to see,
Nature's jest is pure esprit.

In their embrace, humor swells,
As ancient wit through silence dwells.
Among the trees, happiness dwells,
A comedy show, the forest tells.

Murmurs of the Old Ones

Oaks whisper secrets of old,
Tales of mischief, daring and bold.
With acorns and laughter, behold,
Wise ones chuckle, treasures unfold.

"Remember the time we swayed?"
Gnarled hands clasped, they conveyed.
"Caught a breeze, nearly dismayed,
But oh, what fun we made!"

Pine trees nod with sage advice,
Offering roots, both thick and nice.
"Let's not forget, life's a slice,
With every turn, just roll the dice!"

Echoed chuckles fill the glade,
As branches stretch, they serenade.
In the quiet, humor's made,
Among the old, joy won't fade.

In the Presence of Ancient Wood

Underneath the ancient wood,
Time stumbles, feeling good.
With every skip and playful thud,
Nature laughs, as only she could.

Woodpeckers drum up the beat,
While squirrels perform a feat.
Together they dance on their feet,
In this whimsical, leafy retreat.

"Hey, did you hear the one about?"
The trees chuckle, without a doubt.
With laughter rising, so devout,
In this green haven, joy's all about.

Laughter echoes, a vibrant song,
With ancient wisdom, they belong.
In this grove where we are strong,
The humor of wood keeps us lifelong.

Whispers Among Giants

In the shade of giants, whispers play,
Squirrels debate about life's buffet.
One claims it's acorns, the best of all,
While the other insists, it's the apples that call.

Underneath the bark, there's laughter loud,
Critics of the wind, they are quite proud.
"Be still!" they shout, the trees start to sway,
As branches gossip, they dance and sway.

The moss wears glasses, reading the ground,
While mushrooms hold court, none dare make a sound.
All listen closely, the tales of the breeze,
Of silly adventures, and mishaps with bees.

So come join the party, take a seat by the roots,
We'll toast to the critters in funky green boots.
Laughter among the branches, a festivity grand,
In the realm of the giants, let joy take a stand.

Echoes of Ancient Woods

In ancient woods where echoes ring,
The trees chuckle softly, it's a funny thing.
They've seen all the antics of critters in flight,
Like raccoons in tuxedos, what a silly sight!

Acorns are falling like comical rain,
While the owls are hooting their gossip, quite vain.
They wink and they nod as they share their tales,
Of mischievous deer who wear jester's veils.

The breeze carries whispers of pranks in the night,
When foxes play hide and seek with delight.
Hilarious moments 'neath the bright moon's glow,
As laughter echoes, the forest will know.

So take a detour along these paths wide,
Join nature's party, come see, and abide.
You'll find joy aplenty and smiles galore,
In the echoes of woods, life's a comedic roar!

Serenade of the Tall Ones

In a concert hall made of branches so grand,
The tall ones perform with a wobbly stand.
Their roots tap the beat, their leaves sway with cheer,
As the crowd full of critters all gather near.

A raccoon on drums, he's the star of the show,
While squirrels sing harmonies, voices in tow.
An owl's the director, with glasses askew,
"Let's do it again, but with more silly mew!"

The whispering winds join this fanciful song,
Tickling the branches like a breeze all night long.
The tall ones, they dance, with laughter contagious,
In a serenade scene truly outrageous!

So clap your paws together, if you hear a sweet tune,
Let's dance with the tall ones, beneath the bright moon.
In a world of tall trees, where joy never bans,
The serenade lingers, as nature's wild fans.

Shadows of the Timbered Sky

In the shadows where trees touch the sky,
Silly shadows march by, oh my, oh my!
With a hop and a skip, they twist and they twirl,
Creating a dance, oh what a whirl!

The branches lean low, with whispers so light,
As a squirrel with a mustache prepares for flight.
He claims he's the fastest, zooming with glee,
But trips on a twig, oh, how funny to see!

Amongst the tall trunks, there's laughter galore,
With raccoons in capes seeking treasures to score.
A beaver holds court, sharing tales of his fame,
While the turtles just chuckle, "All this is a game!"

So when you stroll through trees, remember this cheer,
Join in with the fun, let go of your fear.
In shadows of giants, let your heart fly high,
With a laugh and a skip, reach for the sky!

Chronicles of the Timbered Realm

In a forest where trees wear their crowns,
The squirrels throw parties and dance all around.
A raccoon with a hat thinks he's quite the king,
While woodpeckers drum up a joyous fling.

An owl in a tux takes a break from his sleep,
To gossip with rabbits who giggle and leap.
The pinecones are talking, they've secrets to share,
Of creatures and magic that vanish in air.

Beneath leafy arches, picnics take flight,
With ants as the waiters till dawn's gentle light.
The fox tells tall tales of treasures and gold,
While trees listen closely, their bark never old.

So cheers to the timbered, their laughter so free,
In a realm filled with wonder and bright jubilee.
With roots intertwined in a comical dance,
In the woods, every creature deserves a chance.

Solace in the Sounds of the Forest

Whispers of branches paint stories galore,
Where crickets compose symphonies, never a bore.
The frogs throw a concert beneath the moonlight,
While fireflies flicker like stars taking flight.

A bear with a ukulele croons in delight,
As hedgehogs tap toes in their spiky invite.
The cows watch enviously from the hilltops,
Wishing for rhythm to borrow from hops.

In this orchestra formed by the rustling leaves,
Each note is a gift, as the forest believes.
The wind joins in laughter, a playful refrain,
As all of creation sings joyously again.

So come hear the laughter, the songs in the air,
It's a comedy show, with nature laid bare!
With spiderwebs glistening, a sparkling stage,
In the heart of the woods, life's a playful page.

Hymns of the Rooted Beings

Under the surface, the roots start to hum,
With fungi that giggle, oh, aren't they fun?
A tree on the corner is cracking a joke,
While mushrooms all chuckle in a fluffy cloak.

The sunbeams break forth, tickling the bark,
As ants play tag, racing through the dark.
Each twig gleefully swings in the breeze,
While laugh echoes softly from trees by the seas.

The hedgehogs recite rhymes in mossy glades,
With a chorus of laughter that never fades.
The laughter of roots, a secretive cheer,
In a home filled with whimsy and joy, oh so dear.

So here's to the beings that giggle below,
In a world where the funniest stories can grow.
With every tight knot in this woodland parade,
The hymns of the rooted sing laughs unafraid.

Fables of Light and Leaf

Once in a glade lived a bold little sprite,
Who'd tickle the branches till day turned to night.
With laughter like sunshine, he flitted about,
Turning dull moments into funny bouts.

A frog in a tux tried to outsmart a fly,
But the frog tripped and fell, oh my, oh my!
The laughter erupted like bubbles in streams,
As friends joined together, creating wild dreams.

A hedgehog recites from a scroll made of bark,
A fable of mischief and larks in the dark.
With mysteries woven in shadows and leaves,
Each tale brings a giggle, oh how it weaves.

So gather 'round closely, dear friends of the wood,
For fables of light offer joy, oh so good.
With every leaf rustle, and every tree sway,
The forest is laughing, so let's join the play.

Nature's Chorus of Eternal Flora

Beneath the boughs where squirrels do dance,
The blossoms giggle at every chance.
A rabbit sings with a funky flair,
While bees do buzz and twirl in the air.

The daisies wear hats, the roses a grin,
Their petals applaud with a cheerful spin.
Even the ferns join in with a sway,
As nature's band plays all night and day.

The banyan tree tells jokes quite tall,
A wise old trunk that has seen it all.
Its branches twist, with laughter they share,
And pinecones chuckle, floating through air.

With roots that laugh and leaves that cheer,
Each critter joins in, year after year.
In nature's concert, all have a part,
A bountiful show, a true work of art.

The Symphony of Tall Shadows

The shadows stretch long, like a silly cat,
They tickle the ground, how about that?
With beams of sunlight dancing around,
The squirrels hold auditions, such joy abound!

The shadows whisper secrets to the breeze,
As ants in a line march with such ease.
The tall trees giggle as tumbleweeds roll,
Creating a scene of comedic strolls.

A crow caws a tune that's out of tune,
While raccoons band together under the moon.
With clapping applause from the leaves up high,
The shadows play games, oh my! Oh my!

In this woodland stage, laughter is gold,
Tales of the trees in their roots unfold.
So join in the fun, under skies so blue,
With shadows and laughter, there's much to do!

Revelations Beneath the Vaulted Foliage

In canopy shades, where secrets reside,
The leaves exchange stories, with joyous pride.
A chipmunk recites poetry in a tree,
While crickets provide a soft symphony.

The light filters through, like confetti in air,
With fronds that whisper, a comedic affair.
The ferns engage in a marvelous play,
While butterflies giggle at mischief on display.

Underneath arches of ever-green lore,
Where laughter erupts from the roots and the core.
The moss takes a nap while wildflowers dream,
Each moment a jest in this natural theme.

So tiptoe and chuckle, you might chance upon,
A stand-up parade of the critters till dawn.
With foliage thick, there's much to admire,
In a world full of glee, where laughter won't tire.

Love's Embrace amidst Swaying Giants

Amidst the titans, tall and grand,
A squirrel proposes with a tiny hand.
In a heart-shaped nest, they spin and twirl,
With blossoms like confetti, love's crazy whirl.

The branches sway gently, like a waltzing pair,
While blossoms blossom, love's sweet affair.
A bunny brings roses, so fresh and bright,
Creating romance under the soft moonlight.

With shadows embracing, the world holds its breath,
As leaves kiss the breeze in a dance of finesse.
The towering giants nod with delight,
To love in the woods, a beautiful sight.

So gather your giggles and toss them around,
In the embrace of nature, true joy can be found.
With whiskers and wings, love's crazy spread,
In every dance, let laughter be wed.

www.ingramcontent.com/pod-product-compliance
Lightning Source LLC
Chambersburg PA
CBHW072136070526
44585CB00016B/1704